AF413173

Created by: Augustus O. Brown Jr.

Published by
JanieMae's Cosmic Garden
Copyright 1/2024

First poem written at 5 years
old. First book written at 40.
Time taken, not wasted.

CREATE.

Message>Grammar

New Scripture

It's been spoken... Been transmitted... Documented and televised...

Well It's a new day baby...
The revolution is being revised.

I am free.

I am we.

Break the curse...
Repeat after me:

No one can take away, what God has given unto me.

My soul, my mind, my body, my time...
My talent... Individuality.

I wake up so blessed.

I carry no stress.

I cherish the temple.

I give me my best.

Up... Up... Up... when I fall.

When I'm down I get back up!

Nobody else on this planet appraises me.

I am a treasure. I am enough.

I am a treasure. I am enough.
I am a treasure. I am enough.

My birthright is up in the mountains...
My birthright is down in the sea...
My birthright is to connect with the earth...
My birthright is peace and prosperity.

I can not be stopped.

I will always win.

I will cherish myself, my family,
My neighbors and my friends.

Up. Up. Up. Is where I'm going...

I rise up.
I play.
I win.

How I Made The Sun Rise

(A whimsical retelling of an uplifting and
enlightening event)

"Did you make the sun rise?"
An unseen passerby asked of me.

I nodded my head in confirmation while proud tears
trickled down my cheeks.

Didn't know I had the power.
Yet, it was so easy to do.

Began my day in gratitude;
This put my vision into clear view.

I started with a,
"Tap"
Then I let out a,
"BANG!"

Pride moved throughout my vessel.
My arms now unrestrained.

Then a
"BOOM! Ba-Ba-Ba-Bap"
Followed by a sweet,
"Ting. Ting."

When I felt the sound vibrating in my body,
a bright smile it did bring.

I glimpsed a peek of sunlight,
It started smiling too.

Now I know what makes it happy;
Just gotta follow through.

I gave a,
"Bibbily ba ba... ta ta...
RING! RING!"

The birds and squirrels gave me praises and
collectively started to sing.

My left foot started tapping.
I threw my shoulders back.

Proud, confident and regal...
Empowered and enlightened,
while watching nature react.

I play harder.
"BOOM-Ba. BOOM-Ba. BOOM-Ba. BOOM-BOOM-
BOOM"
I play softer.
"Tiddly-Ta, Ting-Ting-Ta, Ting-Ting-Ting"

I breathe light. I breathe deep.

I drop my head and close my eyes...
I find inner peace in my own beat.

When I lift my eyes to the heavens,
I'm moved by a surprise...

An orange star dazzling high in a pink sky!

That's how I made the sunrise.

Only had to show up.
Only had to be the best me.

When I use my gifts for GOoD...
There are no impossibilities.

Ashé

Can you use it in a sentence?

A loner can still be romantic

Hedonistic heart breaker
Problematic & pedantic

Learned the last word from a cartoon show

Do I sound smart?
Do you like my rhythmic flow?

My daddy man wanted me to expand
my vo cab u lary

My mama taught me to spell...
Still didn't win the spelling Bee

Just a silly clown full of childish antics

Did I use it right?

I'm still talking bout pedantic

Stay Down

I fell again...

I fell for me

Fell for the beauty and intelligence that sometimes I can't see

I fell in love...

This love has set me free
This love revived my smile...

Love of my kinks, love of my quirks and love of all my eccentricities..

I touched a body

The body belongs to me

My body is grand...
My body is sexy...

My body gets me everywhere I need me to be

Everything about me is great.

No matter what I wear; No matter what I ate

It matters how I feel. It matters how I think.

This day is MINE.

I am balanced. I am in sync.

WHAT Do You LOVE ABOUT You?

FOUR M'S TO FACILITATE A BETTER DAY, LIFE, AND ALL-AROUND BETTER YOU!

MEDITATION

That voice that tells you, "YOU AIN'T SHIT," needs to be shut down! Quiet your mind for a few minutes before you start your day. Remind yourself that you ARE the shit!
Breathe in...
Breathe out... Nice.

MoASTURBATION

A healthy sex life starts and finishes with you. Shared pleasure is great, but gratifying yourself is powerful. Rub one out... Make yourself shout! I recommend doing it before you log into any dating app. Thank me later when you're NOT waking up next to a stranger that smells like ham. You're welcome.

MOVEMENT

Do something physical (or just masturbate again)! Starting the day with exercise has so many benefits for your body and mind. You'll probably eat better too. Twerk in the mirror for 10 minutes before you shower.
*BOUNCE! BOUNCE!
Dat azz looks good.

Manifestation

How are you going to get to a destination without a roadmap? Don't say a GPS! Smart ass...

Writing down what you want to accomplish, saying it out loud, adding action to your words; These are the first steps to attaining your goals. Something about putting it on paper makes magic happen. Trust me. Try it.

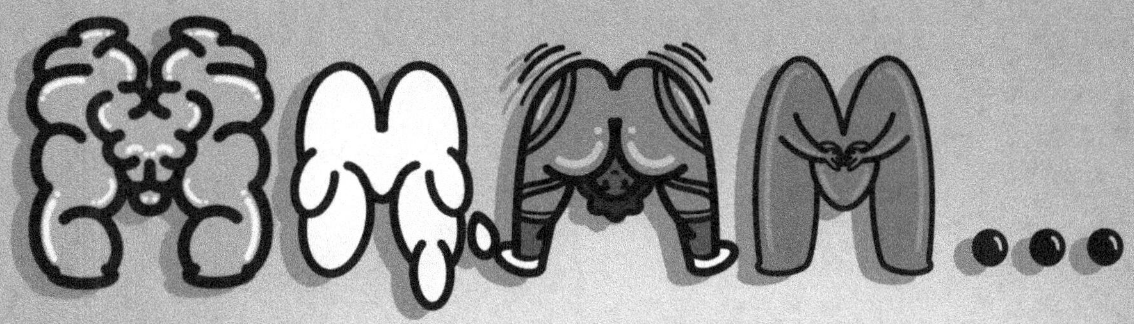

What a great start to the day!
I failed to mention that you will probably need to wake up about a hour earlier to tackle these four tasks. Before you write me off, aren't you worth it? Perhaps you could wake up at the same time. Just borrow the hour from the time you spend observing other people's lives on Instagram, Facebook and TikTok. This is for YOU! Try it for a week and examine how you feel. If there is a general improvement, great. If your life spirals...
I'm not a licensed anything (other than a driver), and you can't hold me liable for anything.
Have a great day!

What To Do?
(Song)

People dying EVERYWHERE.

Bombs and mines
How can I care...

When I don't... know how... to help?

Children, elders starving every night.
Wronged by blood, now that ain't right.

How can I care...
When I don't... know how to help?

Give my money?
I ain't got none.
Should I stay depressed?
And avoid all fun?
How can I fix an intentionally broken system?
Use my voice? But no one is listenin...
. . .
I will do the right thing right where I'm at.

It's ok to observe before I react.

A lot of people talk but a few people do.

What help do you need?
How can I show up for you?

Revolution

Woke up
Never left the bed

Suns up
Streets running red

Times up
Help outside the head

Fed up?
Activate instead.

I
Will
Do
Better!

Chirp Chirp Chirp

(Song)

Three little birds appeard to me...

They told me not to worry and to let my mind fly free

Pull myself together, shine my crown and do my best

Give thanks to the most high

Play, eat and rest

They tell me,
"Don't give up!"

They tell me to,
"Stand Strong!"

Trust upon my heart
It will never lead me wrong

They tell me
"Don't give in!"

They remind me that
I am the win

Outside love is great
First, I must be my own best friend.

Three little birds appeard to me...

Three little birds set me free.

The Formula
(Song)

I've been grinding every day
I've been hustling every night

Now I know that it's my turn
And I know Im gonna be alright

Still, Sometimes I can get down
But I never count me out

I got God, luck and the universe

So there's no room for doubt

I got God, luck and the universe

Watch my blessings sprout

EVERYTHING I NEED IS ALREADY MINE.
EVERYTHING I WANT WILL BE HERE IN TIME.

Logic

"Nothing new under the sun"
I've heard some people say.

What about this moment?

What about today?

What about growth and opportunities?

What about visions and dreams?

There is always something new…
No matter how it seems.

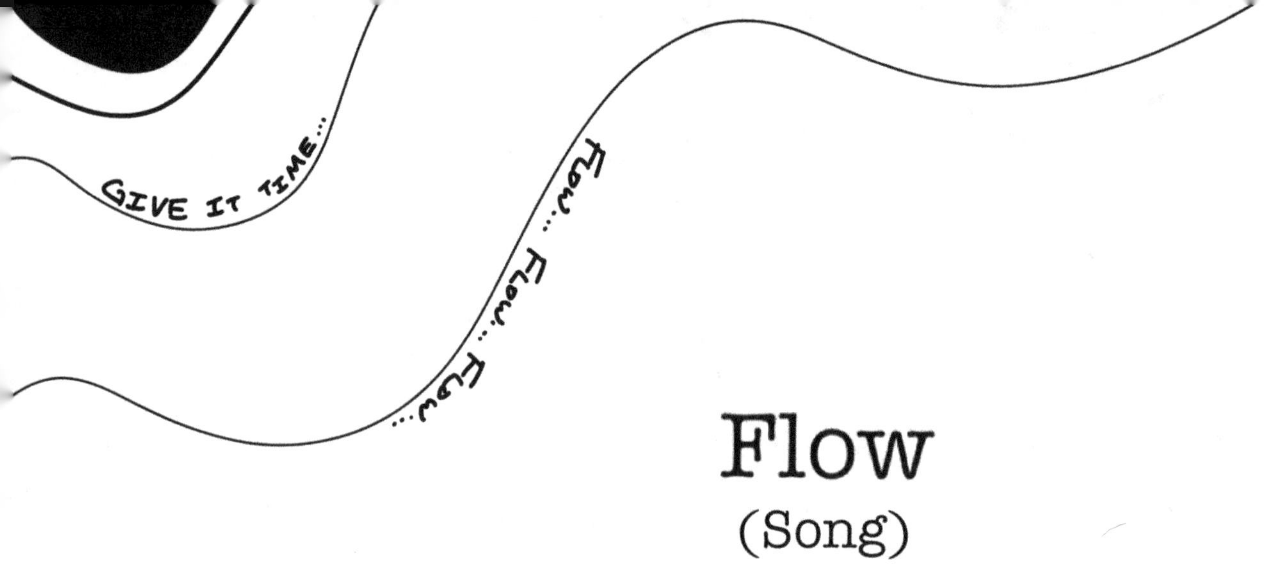

Flow
(Song)

You know what it be?
That way sometimes.

Take a few breaths and I will be just fine.

Keep moving forward. Stay in touch with my mind.

Loving and living is how I'm using my time.

Got Me Itching

Ants in a bed...

Building castles in our heads...

Soon under water...
Soon all dead.

Hurry. Hurry. Hurry.
Walk. Run. Scurry.

All come in different.
All leave the same.

Only reason we cry is because we know we soon die.

Owe it to existence to try.

WRITE · DOODLE · MANIFEST

Your pink puff...

It hangs in clear sight

I should throw it away.
That just doesn't feel right

Tea tree and lavender scented memories of soapy
soapy circles
made by my hands on your back...

I pull you in closer
Blessed suds travel down your crack

Fuck this pink puff!

And fuck you too!
Fuck this separation!
And fuck all that we've been through!

It wasn't all you

It was me too.

I can take the blame...
That was difficult for you to do.

That stupid pink puff

Pink like your lips

Gazing into your eyes
My logic stumbles and slips

Farewell pink puff.

Time to move on.

One last whiff...
"Aaaaaaaah"
Damn! The feelings still ain't gone...

The Hypnotic Cutie

Smoky skin

Rhythmic bounce

The sight of you just got me high

No need to buy an ounce

Normal

Kinky
Freaky
Nasty

Been described as one or three

Explorer
Tactile
Lover

My true identity

Searching for a hidden treasure with alchemic energy

No clothes, or inhibitions
Nature designed me to be free.

Why mask? Why hide?

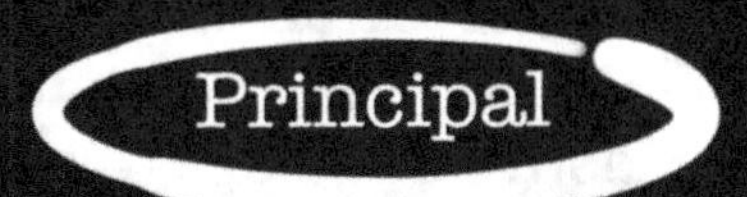

Please, pleaser...
Please them real good.

Give the people what they want

Make them feel like they should.

Please, please pleaser...
Always wear a smile.

There is no time to be down

Just pretend to be someone else, pull it together...
That reasoning is sound.

Please, please pleaser...
Pick yourself up.

Give a little more...

Your good is ok... But that shit ain't good enough.

Please, pleaser...
Maybe you need a rest.

Maybe it's time to please the pleaser...

In self pleasure, please invest.

Prayer Hands Emoji
Down on my luck
Unsure of where to go

My intelligent friend...
Who doesn't understand no

First responder skills
An unwelcome mouth to mouth

My body hits the floor...
Your mouth moves further south

Rotten tooth monster, Christ on your lips

Lies in your eyes

Demons possess your mind and your hips

How could this happen?

I thought I was free

Share my pain with a friend

"I still absolutely adore him" are the words she says to me.

Bury that shit.
Hide it deep away.
Nobody gives a fuck.
Pretend I'm ok.

Can't stop reliving it.

I thought I was free

Body taken by a brother
It no longer belongs to me.

We Need Your Support

Flags a waving

Horns a honkin

Plenty people passing by

Candidates and home team fanfare seem the same

I go hmmm... and wonder why?

Anyone can sell a shiny dream

Change is constant even if it don't seem

Folk say don't throw your vote away

What do I do when I don't believe a word folk say?

Campaign money could help somebody
Global warming is such a hottie

Bumper stickers change the world

Fuck so and so
Nonsense about this and that

I wonder if anyone on the ballot cares about exactly where I'm at?

Do they care about what I think?

Do they know what I need?

It all feels like a silly game that's based on self importance and greed

Up the hill and off the cliff

I'll follow.

You take the lead.

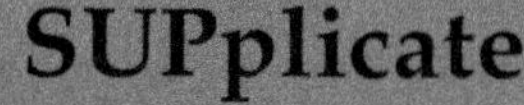

SUPplicate

Your god can talk to me

Come hear what he got to say

Give me some money

I can show you how to pray

Give me some money

I can show you how to shout

Give me your attention
Let me take away your doubt

Salvation for sale

Just do what I say
I mean, it's coming from your god

But he can't talk to you today

Give me some money

Gotta fuel up my jet

I'm flying to see your god

Tell him I said, 'hi,'

Ok, bet.

I WALKED TO MY SECRET ISLAND
I EXPOSED MY SECRET PARTS
ENGAGED IN A SECRET FEAST
RELEASED ALL IN MY SECRET HEART

MADE A PUBLIC PACT WITH SELF...
OH SO SECRETLY

MY LOVE OF SELF IS NO SECRET
THIS DECLARATION HAS SET ME FREE

Classified Information

Second sister said I'm somewhere on the spectrum

Lusted after lover said my neurons got that spice

Maybe I am...
What if it do?

What does it change?
What's it to you?

Society says I'm on a rainbow spectrum

The range is ultraviolet to red

Can't I just be a colorful character?

My worth ain't defined by how I get down in my bed

Skin is decadent pure cocoa on the brown spectrum

Application try to dumb me down to flat "Black"

Why every nuance need a box?

All these fuckin spectrums are WHACK!

TO DO LIST

BE A DOPE ASS MOTHERFUCKER

THE NOW IS TRUE. INVESTIGATE. DO.

What's the word?

Special is not special enough.

Sexy... Too one dimensional.

When I think to describe you, I need something
more appropriate to say.

Your energy is delicious.

Your intellect; So intriguing.

Splendiferous you are in every possibly
conceivable way.

A body built by beauty... Brick by brick.

Patience be a pal...
Do not let me come too quick.

Thank you for splendiferously blessing my
morning view.

The sunrise now has competition thanks to the
magnanimously splendiferous you.

Up LooK

My view ain't so bad

Stopped thinking bout what I had

My gifts are for me
Sometimes need help to see

Seen the world from under the sea
And over the clouds

When the voices in my head stop being so loud
I realize...

My view ain't so bad.

Not my last

Huevos on the ground

Count them...
Uno... Dos... Three

"Can I get your cart...
I got no quarter on me."

No to the quarter dollar.

No to your request.

I'm in my asshole era

Gotta do my best

Boundaries matter even in the least

No feels good.

No is a release.

Directions

Don't know where I'm going

Know where I stand

Do my best to chart the route but I can't control the plan

Blowing with the breeze

Ever changing seasons champion my command

Don't know where I'm going

Know where I stand

I'm here
In this very moment

I'm here

Deeper

I dipped my toe
I like your flow

Can I dive in?

Will you let go?

It's safe to swim

Let's catch a wave

Float with my love

True Love can save.

So much sand all around
you're the only treasure I see...

If you think I move too fast...
Take a deep breath and catch up to me

Lauderdale Lavandaria

Wheels been spinning all day

Just took a break to put my fly on the spin cycle

Every day feels the same
That's why I been wearing the same rags for the last three days

Credit of three
Wash for free

Feeling kinda dusty

Gotta pay for the dry

Plastic bottle of Chardonnay from the people without shoes

Duchess made bun
Honey is ingredient 21 down

I still chew

Got some queso chip cuz... wine & cheese
Duh

I got class

Been four years without draws on my ass

Tomorrow I'll be fresh
In the morning I'll be clean

For now, I'm jammin to my funk
Inhale myself and dream

Puppy Play
(Song)

I'm a funky dog
A nasty dog

A crafty dog that likes to play and roam

A dog that will lay up under you
And nap all day when I'm home alone

I'm a dog that chases the cat, the bone sometimes my own
tail too

I'm a horny dog that wants to hump every time I lay my
puppy dog eyes on you

Woof! Woof!

I'm a greedy dog that wants my treats, my food, your food
and my chew toy too

So let me sniff that rump
Then imma take a dump and run around the park for an
hour or two

Woof! Woof!

He's a wild thang!!!

Let me smell your animal

Give me the growl of your beast

You without your domestication is a delight and a
refreshingly welcomed treat

I will breathe in your hind
I answer your call to the wild with no delay

Viewing you in your creature form leaves me engorged,
beguiled and excited for the journey that is today

You say to answer the door naked

Gladly, I oblige

Darkness inches away from the morning as I watch you pass by where I reside

Let out a whistle to change your direction

A few minutes later, you've incited an erection

You got something that I want
A few things that a man like me needs

The want to be wanted

The need to be pleased

Activated inner springs
Moans and slaps

My stomach growls...

What a symphony

Laying here
Wondering why I seek unsatisfying options to nourish me

Always back to hungry

Thoughts go back to the darker side

Morning lift me up with the sun

Self, please remind me of other ways to have fun

More options for fulfillment
Ways to abate my gluttony

Take me to the water
Wash me in the sea

Black Coffee Jingle
(Song)

Let me stand back...
Imma watch you drip
*snap
Up & ready for a taste,

Got me biting on my lip.

Fill it to the top
(Ooh)
Take it to the tip

Never let me down

Always ready for a sip

So legit
I can't quit

Let me have another taste

Feel your heat radiating from your vessel to my face

WooSah

WooSah

WooSah

Let me stand back...
Imma watch you drip

So rich. So smooth.
Black Coffee always hits!

AAAAH

ABUNDANCE

Possibilities are nice.

Moments are real.

I be feeling myself...
Smelling myself...
Telling myself that I'm great

It doesn't matter what I bring to the table...

I'm still showing up with my plate.

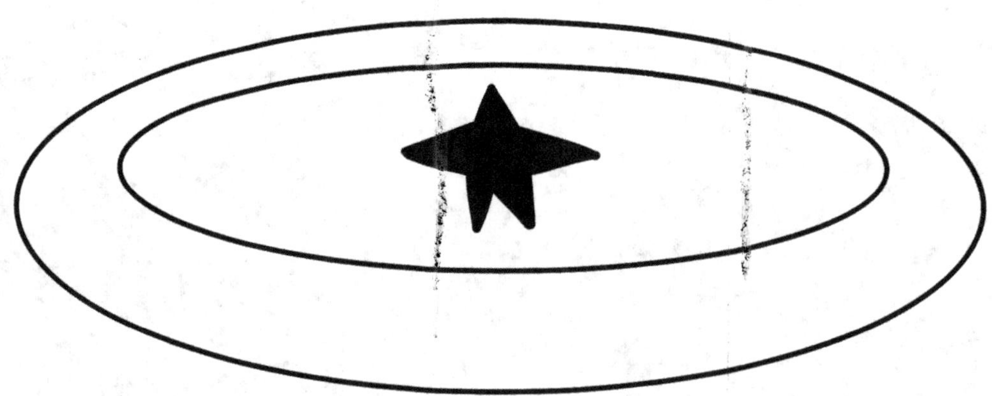

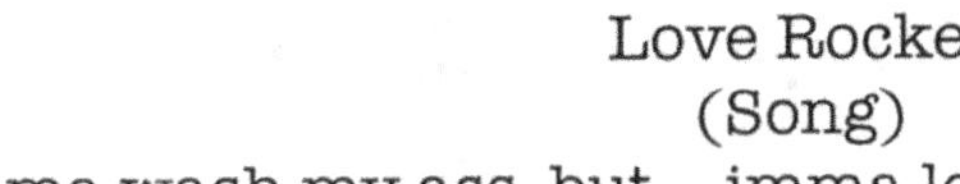

Love Rocket
(Song)
Imma wash my ass, but… imma leave these balls sweaty.

Come and get this funky feast.
Two meatballs; Don't need no skettie.

Certified angus beef.
You don't need a spork.

Will you be my tenderoni?
Trying to stay away from pork.

Then we fire off into the future…
You can call me Mr. Sprocket.

Will you leave your world behind and hop on my love rocket?
Rocket
Rocket
Rocket
Rock it!

A love rocket…
Built for you and me.

No need for…
Fuel. You're my energy.

Let's fly higher…
Away from humanity.

I'll terraform you.
I will spray your surface with my seed.

Aww skeet skeet.

"YOUR BOOTY ON MY BEARD"
The ADDICKTIVE
New Fragrance From
AUGUSTUS

"Going Deep"

My eyes are blessed by your beauty. I'm in awe of your
darkness and light

Your scent leads my nose on an adventure. Every inhale...
a ritualistic delight

I'm a tactile being. It's easy to get lost in the feel of your
parts

Booty is my favorite meal, but it's trumped by the taste of
your metaphorical heart

When you say my name, the sound of your voice brings
me to full attention

You are a lover like no other. I'll take a one way ticket to
the depths of your inner dimension

Peace. Good lovin. Prosperity.

COLOR ME.

Ching a ling a ling a ling ding ding
(Song)

I can hear them gold coins

Generational curse breaker

I attract abundances

I'm a money maker

Prosperity and peace and love

Grateful to the most high

My blessings come down from above

I stay winning.
Damn, I'm so fly.

Country boy

You roll your eyes

I blow my breath

The day is long. Life is tough.

Do we still have any love left?

I say your name

You turn around slow

No matter what it is...
Don't care where we are...

This I want you to know...

Before the sun goes down and the moon goes up on this
warm September day

You are my everything

That's what I have to say

So, before we close our eyes, can I see one more of your
bright smiles shining through?

Can I be your everything?

Will you let me love on you?

HUMILITY IS
NOT IN MY NATURE.

HOMO ERECTUS TOLD
ME TO STAND UPRIGHT.

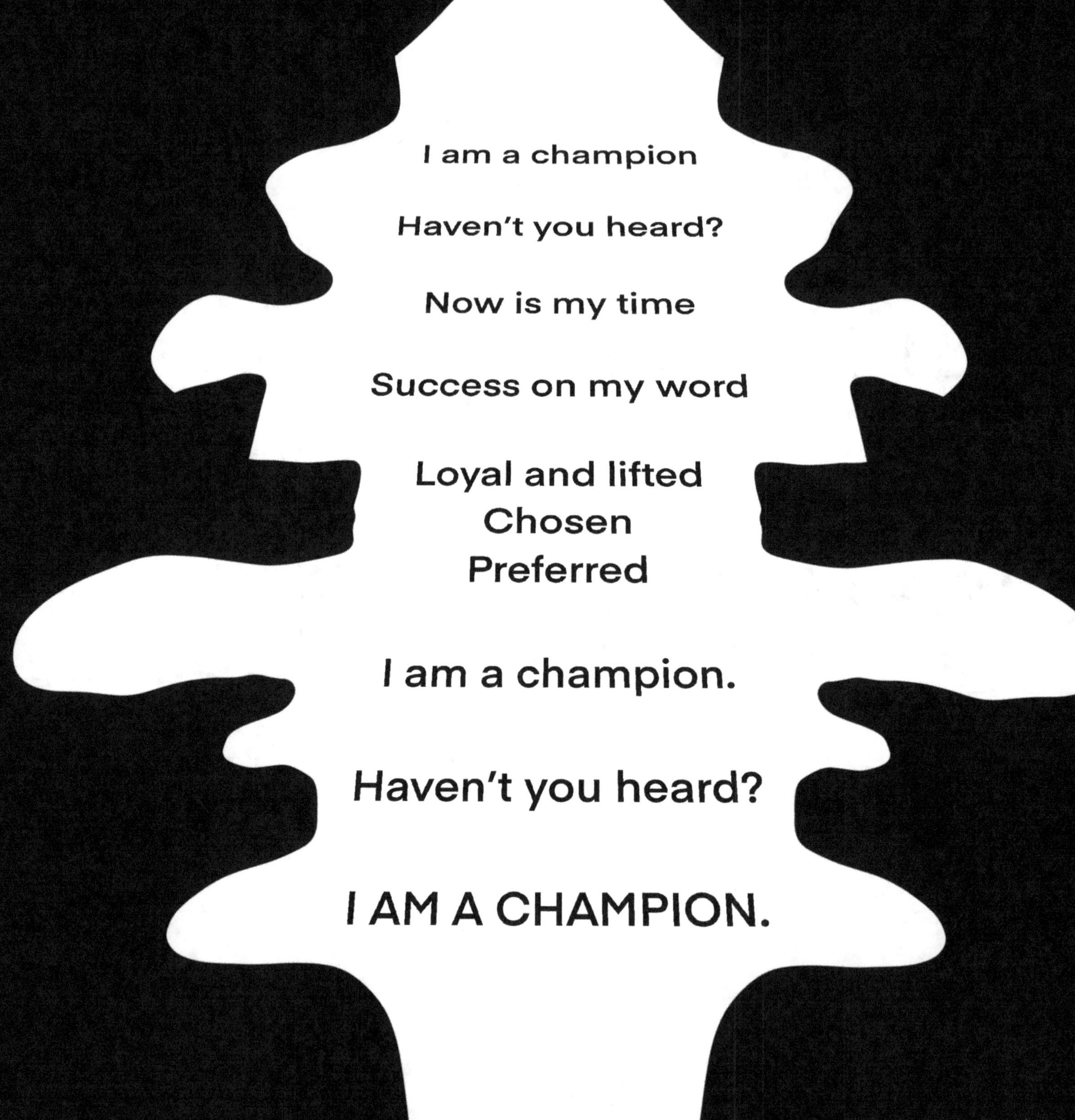

I am a champion

Haven't you heard?

Now is my time

Success on my word

Loyal and lifted
Chosen
Preferred

I am a champion.

Haven't you heard?

I AM A CHAMPION.

Five Letter Fail

Sorry sorry
sorry
Sorry sorry sorry

Sorry

So sorry

The more I say it...

The sorrier I sound

Sorry
So sorry

I'm sorry sorry sorry sorry

Sorry
It's the easiest excuse I found

So easy just to say sorry
Don't need to say anything else

Sorry
So sorry

Sorry is easier than working on self

Sorry

I will use an hour of my day to make sure I am ok.

A stranger's story

Girl, I'm on the way

Later than usual
You know how I do

Friend, I'm on my way to see you

Had to get myself together before I could come through

Quiet on the car ride over

Not sure if this is an Uber or a Lyft

I've been thinking on the car ride over...

Won't lie; I don't want to do this shit

The doors lock up at eight

Feeling a little heavy and we both know why

The whole neighborhood is wrapped around the building

Some people laugh. Other folks cry

Then I see that sad silver Caddy by the front door as I pull
up at seven fifty nine

Sister, I ain't ready to see you like this...

I ain't ready for that last time goodbye

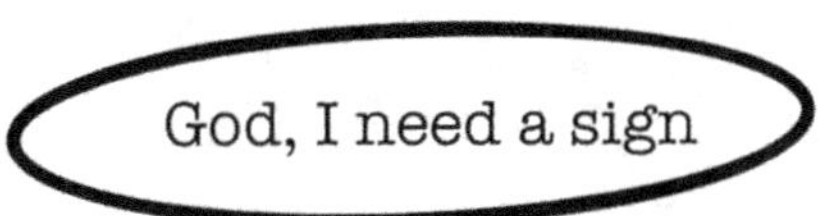

A cardboard sign that says, "Thank you to the cheerful
givers."

Out of cash. Hopefully this banana and a honest smile will
suffice

She says the sheriff locked up her love for 45 whole days.

It's day six; Unsure of how she'll make it without him in
her sight

She apologizes for the tears rolling down her weathered
cheeks

Not in the same shoes but I think I can understand

A prayer for peace slips out of my half parched lips

God, if you're listening, we both could use your hand

Left leg swollen for the past two days or three

Exhausted from driving strangers, but money is tighter
than tight

Polite passengers compliment me on my pretty blue ride…

Pride won't let me say that it's my home tonight

God if you're listening I could use a sign today

Trying to keep my pieces together as one,

Show me a path to my big picture and I will walk that
way…

I could use some rest, and just maybe… a little fun

Convince Store Chronicles

A full bright smile on a dirt decorated face

Pride that beams with no shame
He found treasure in an unexpected place.

While excavating through someone else's trash,

A piece of paper was found worth twenty five cash

No shame in looking where others throw away

Thank you for your story
You made a stranger smile today.

"Ghost"

Thought I was rejected

Realized I've been protected

What is mine finds its way to me

Sweet serendipity

Vivid blue and pink merge on her eyelids

Purple punch is painted precisely on her sweet lips...

She said you have to do something to stand out when you get to
an age as old as this.

Golden filagree dangling down from both ears

Gold and copper butterflies dancing in her salt and pepper hair...

Your vessel may be aged
Your movements a little slowed...

When I take you in, I see beauty everywhere.

WRITE ME A POEM:

I FORGIVE
ME

Breathe

Been up in my feelings
Time to get down and deal

Take a few intentional breaths
Take some time to heal

Won't work myself up
On a break. I'm on chill.

Focused on this moment
It's the only one that's real.

Red Tide Boogie Beatdown on God

(Song)

Island boy
Was locked on land

Needed sunlight
Give him sand

Ocean water
Let it flow

Never dry up
Never let it go

Dance on golden brick paved streets

Life is tasty. Life so sweet.

**Boogie! Boogie!
Move your feet!**

Take a deep breath and find the beat!

Friction… Fire… Create heat

Burn it down. Celebrate their defeat.

Use their ashes… Something new grow.

Unless we try, we never know…

Defeat evil. Defeat hate.

We deserve peace and food on our plate.

Time to rest and meditate

Ok to say NO and show up late

Carry on, everything alright…

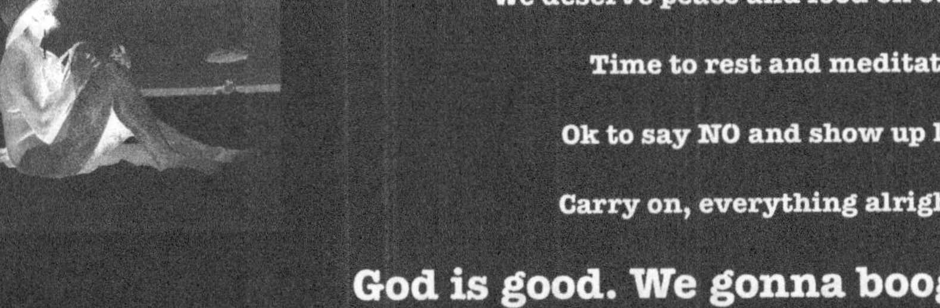

God is good. We gonna boogie tonight!

Shifting
(Song)
I caused a rift

Little ole me divided the sea

A father's love comes with conditions

Broke my mother's heart when I decided to be me

Cut me off and cast me away

I am sick
I'm a disease

A dog with no chain
A bird with no cage

Had to learn how to run and fly free

Love still in my heart

What's broken can be rebuilt

Only feel peace
Only speak blessings

Wont judge myself with guilt

Smile can't be contained

Stepped outside of my own brain

Found my own beat
Started moving my feet

Now I boogie on my new terrain

All doors don't open to all black faces

Please welcome me brother into your prestigious black spaces

White isn't the only threat to black

That's not where the problems begin

Some enemies come from the same struggle

Some enemies wear the same skin

You see me outside brother

Brother, let me in.

"Mama's Boy"

Gaea brought forth beauty from chaos

You did too

That beauty was cradled until he didn't believe just like you.

The winds blew harder without your protection

Every season so harsh

Spring was not the renaissance that was expected

Summer lacked rays

Autumn leaves left without notice

Winter brought no snow

Then...

Rains came in spite of your intentional drought

Your thick shade became inconsequential

The sun shone throughout

Roots fed by love

Nature nurtured when you neglected

Now...

Branches reach out

Roots run deep

Your sapling is tall
Strong
Unbreakable

Actions fueled by confusion no longer test its resilience

Bark that thickened over time protect the still tender flesh

Love blossoms in perpetuity

Refusal to believe your apathy came from contempt

From blame, you are exempt

This fruit might have fallen far from the tree

He grew nonetheless

Black Bunny

Neo didn't make the jump at the beginning

He still ended up being the one

Even though you're going through it

Your race can still be won

You got problems

I got problems

Yours are no worse than mine

Focus on what you can do

Everything will be just fine

Fine, not perfect

What do you expect?

No one makes it out alive

So while you have the gift of life

Strive
Rise
Thrive

No guarantee of tomorrow

Fear is not your friend

It's the enemy that makes you hold your gifts deep within

Share that shit

Time to break free

Worship yourself

Turn off the tv

The people you idolize are no better than you

Focus on your blessings

Not on what you can't do

An original

You can't be replaced

FIRST I SPEAK IT . . .
THEN, I WILL SEE.
I GET WHAT I WANT.
I ALWAYS HAVE WHAT I NEED.

The elusive mango evades me yet again

Sweet
Firm yet soft

Ripe
All the way ready

Drippin... juicy... at its peak
Core, sturdy and steady

So indulgent
I can't speak

Mango so good that I forsake refined sugars because you make me feel alright

Sweet sweet mango...
My delicious delayed delight.

Ban-A-Rrific

Bans on books
No ban on guns

When is the last time a book shot up a school or church?

How about a ban on low pay for hard work?

Rent goes up
Pay goes down

Ban inflation all around

Bans on bodies

Bans on rights

Band together
Time to fight

Two days since you've been gone

I've used your towel each and every one

Our scents merged together

I don't want that part to be done

Laying around with you is always fun

Anime
Syfy
And dancing

These are a few of your favorite things

I fall asleep with your head of curly hair resting on my belly

You have no idea how much joy it brings

The feeling of being loved
Hell, even being liked

Fear of not possessing this has kept me up on many nights

Those nights have passed

They're gone, just like you

I'll hold on to your towel

Sweet aromatic memories woven into a shade of deep blue

It's me
(Song)
Won't deny that I can be moody as fuck

I ain't getting laid
Barely getting paid

Selling my dreams for a buck

Every morning I wake up with a new attitude

So give me a break if in this moment... I seem kind of rude

It's nothing to do with you
And everything to do with me

Just back the hell up
&
Let me breathe
&
Let me be

In a few minutes, I'll probably dig up a smile

But, it's been a long day, so it might take me awhile.

Good God...
It's been a long day, so it might take me awhile.

Damn!
I
LOOK
GOOD!

Beating yourself up is the same as self tenderization. It makes it easier for others to devour you.

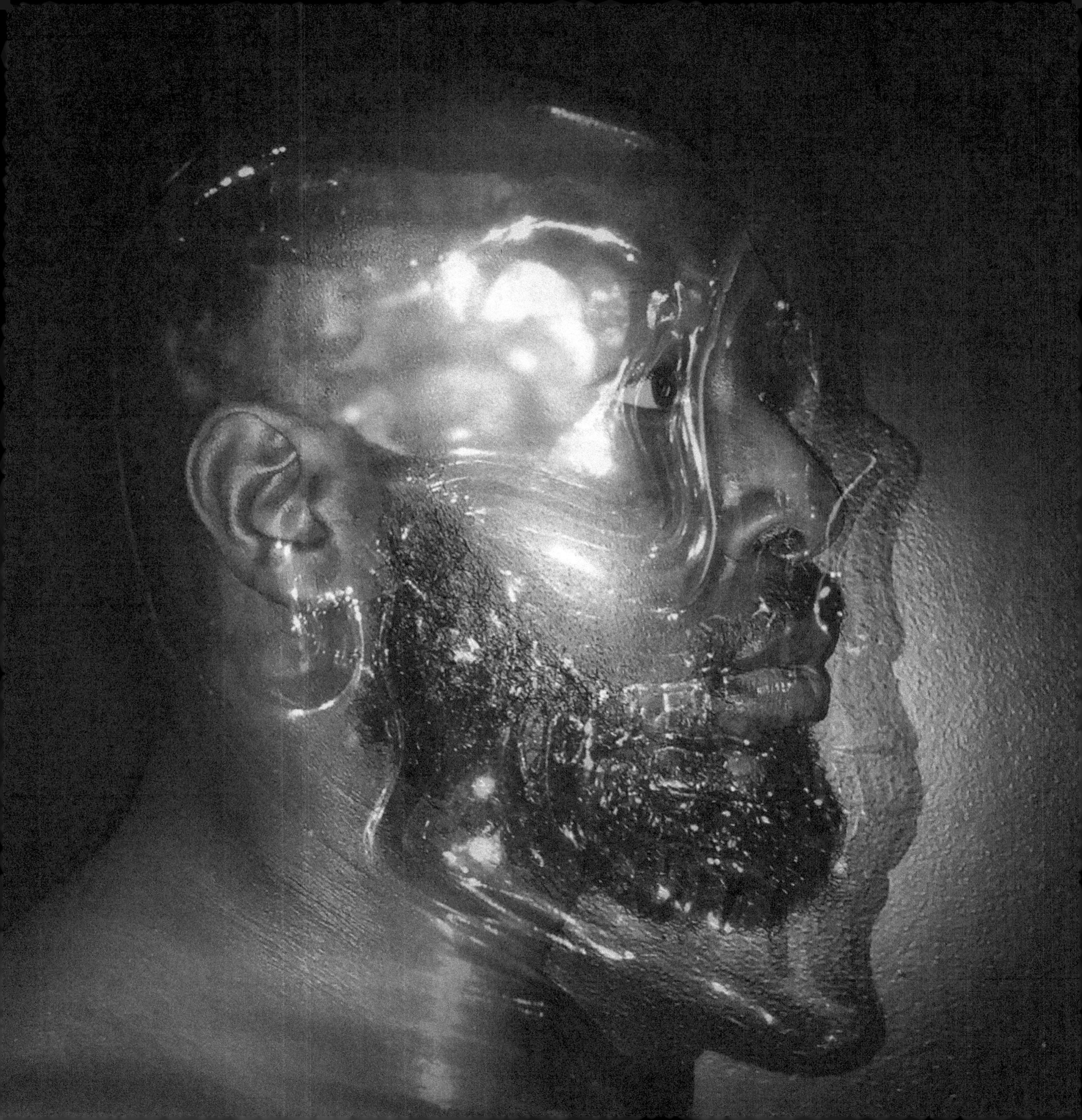

Different Angle

Sometimes it's hard to look

Sometimes I look away

The mirror

An ally

An adversary, often times more

I think everyone is great

I say that everyone is strong

When I look at myself...

I see

WRONG!
WRONG!
WRONG!

Ok, chill

I know it's not true

Ugly Blues

Laying in bed listening to the sounds of the city

All of the people I see all look so rich and pretty

I wonder what does it feel like to have shit together

I wonder will it take for me to get better

They say hard work pays
Wonder why I'm so broke

Laugh at myself
Fell like a mother fuckin joke

Saw kids fighting with an old man in the street

Kept on moving. Didn't say a peep.

This world ain't mine
Heard it's up in the devil's hands

Where is god?

Don't think I can comprehend

So many pretty faces moving through the busy city

So down and out

Feeling kinda shitty.

Thirsty for ME
(Song)
I've been a little parched

Oh yeah, a nigga been in heat

Don't need PornHub or Twitter…

I'm going to masturbate to ME

Turned on by my scent and my sexy body

Won't visualize another

ME is all I see

A sexier motherfucker ain't never been made

Skin glows so bright

Stays resistant to the shade

Booty on juicy

Like a blackberry lemonade
(Aye)
Dick at attention
Like it's ready to invade

Sexy and special from my dome down to my feet

Treating myself kindly,
But bout to beat up on my meat

Won't ignore that prostate
It was put there as a treat

Feeling like a meal
Provecho, Bon Appétite
(Aye)
Bon Appétite
(Aye)
Bon Appétite

Gotta lick my lips because I'm looking so sweet

After, take a nap
Once I go skeet skeet

Wipe myself down so I don't have to wash the damn sheets

Beach Bum Blues

A place to shower...
A bed in which to sleep...

Best things are free, but living ain't cheap.

12 hours a day
Still, the back seat is where I lay

Stay on the move so they can't take my ride away.

Everything behind
Everything late

I refuse to go hungry,
So, motherfucker, wait

I know there is a light

I know this ain't my end

Until I find my way out... I'll dream. I'll pretend.

A Isabela

You gave me so much

I took even more away

Left my earthly possessions,
Because I know I will come back some day

Some day soon.

No true concept of self love before

You taught that to me

You helped me see my body differently

You reminded me of my link to the sea

-Sandia y luz solar-

I didn't always understand your language,
But, you took your time with me.

Didn't want to leave

Wish I never did...

Unlike any other, you held me down

Lost on an island with no desire to be found

Feeling It
(Song)

Do your own dance,
March to your own beat

Got worries in your head?
Well, work them out with your feet

You can slide, bouce, shake,
Do whatever feels right

Push the dark clouds away,
Time to welcome in the light

Tension in your shoulders?
Shake it out one time

Let the stress go
While you do a durty wine

This aint a challenge,
It's your right to do you

Keep your eyes to the sky
Now, watch your dreams come true

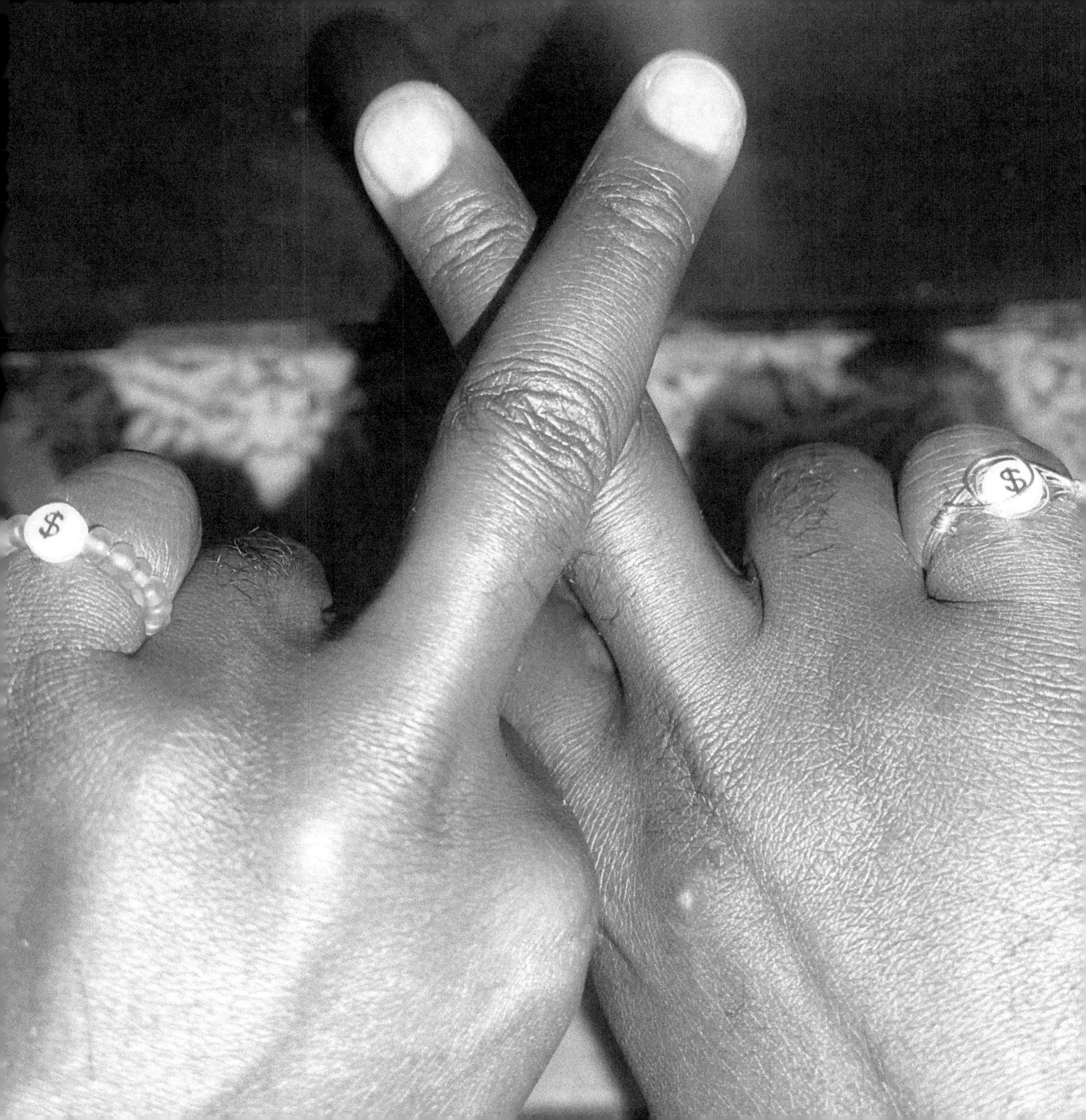

WRITE · DOODLE · MANIFEST

The waves are tall. Taller and more assertive than I've ever observed. The sand is rough. The roughest I've ever felt. The height and texture excite me. I am ready to play.

There is a young couple sitting at the oceans edge. They see me. I see them. Neither of us speak. Eye contact is an exchange that I find more telling than polite pleasantries.

I look at the horizon line where sky greets sea. There is a north to south rainbow that kisses the water's surface on both ends. The center is obstructed by smoky grey fog. It was raining a few moments ago. Now the sun flirts with the clouds. I am sitting directly center of this colorful phenomenon. Science explains how a rainbow works. I'm too simple to comprehend. It is inexplicably majestic and splendiferous to my naive, child like eyes. This technicolored portal whispers, "Boy, get in."
I obey.

The waves are playful.
They take no time to put me in my place, which is apparently the sea floor. The sand drops off quickly. There is no shallow zone. My feet are scratched by the textured earth beneath them as the water flows to and fro. Towering and curling rushes of the most serene hued aquamarine waves bring me to and leave me in awe. White fluffy caps wash over my head. The motion is beautifully violent. Somewhat fear inspiring. Yet, I laugh a kids laugh with every tooth in my head on display. Joy runs throughout my body. This is the first time I've been happy in days.

The waves are exhausting.
After about ten minutes of playing with the God of the sea, I tap out and take to dry land. The young couple has drifted down the beach to my rainbow portal. They look at me with kind and questioning eyes. I still do not speak. Instead, I dig a hole and bury myself chest deep. The abrasive nature of the sand combined with its wet weight, forces me to sit in place and look to the sea. Uncomfortable and effective. I can finally breathe.

Speckled grains of all shades cover my deep brown body. So deep brown that it was the darkest shade of creaseless concealer at Sephora. I was curious as I waited on an associate to locate a gift set that I was scheduled to deliver. My ego swelled seeing a cosmetic that was deep enough to compete with my complexion, but failed in comparison to my multidimensional, silky epidermis. The associate returned from her quest unsuccessful. She uttered, "I'm so sorry." I asked her why she was sorry and began to preach that saying, 'I'm sorry" is the same as saying I am worthless and of no value. She looked at me with large golden brown eyes that appeared to be confused and understanding. She smiled and thanked me. Me and my dark chocolate, competition winning skin went on our way. A way that would lead us to a refracted portal, covered nipple high in rough sand, watching tall waves crash.

The waves are powerful.

The crystal clear waters have gone murky

Once, I could see my feet
Now there is no clear way

Clouds conceal the stars in a warm March sky

Guess I'll have to wish on the moon today

Am I depressed?

Thumb hovering over send
My therapist would be mortified
Message says "I miss you"
Another line about how hard I know you tried

Did you really?
Are my memories correct?
Is the cold making me lonesome?
What are these feelings of regret?

Please don't do it
Don't carry it out
It's not the right move
So,why so much doubt?

The rain hits my cheek
Or was that a tear?
I know that I miss you
Loneliness is an even bigger fear

I've met others
None of them are you
I've laid with others
I couldn't follow through

So many things I want to say

I don't want this toxic cycle to begin
Again
And again

Just like the agains before

If I hit send today
Tomorrow I'll show up at your door

You'll say you love me
I'll say I love you
We'll never do this again
The words won't be true

Maybe next life time
Or maybe next year
Maybe it'll be never
I know my love will still be here

Delete message
Delete contact too
Delete these feelings

That's the hardest part to do

Sand Dollar Serenade

I have been searching low for you, my treasure

High time for you to present yourself to me

When can I wrap my arms around you my lover?

This question circles my head on repeat

Take your place beside me
Let the prophecy be fulfilled

Why hide yourself any longer?
Let your beauty be revealed

This place has worn me down

Fighting all sorts of evil

Please don't leave me here alone

My only mission, your safe retrieval

Blessed with many gifts
Nothing more special than my love for you

You have the gift of manifestation
Come to me. Make my dream come true

It was written in the cosmos

The message came on a shooting star

That is why I watch the heavens

Don't know if you're near. Hope you are not far.

Forsook my exalted existence

Chose to walk amongst the men

So many cold, unfeeling creatures

Often my patience wears thin

You are the missing piece

Once you join me, we take to the clouds

Can you hear my call sweet one?

Daily I sing your song aloud

Willing to explore the depths

Open a portal in the middle of the sea

State my intention on a rainbow

Just reveal yourself to me

Patience is a virtue

More of a villain the way I see

Heart is beating to your celestial tune

Pray every night that you will join me soon

Then back through the clouds together

Together, peace in paradise shall resume

"Bibbly ba ba da"

Gladys Bentley growling

Birds chirping in the back

Calm waters flow ahead

Chill. Don't react.

Rest is owed

Never feel it's earned

Yesterday is history

Today comes with new lessons learned

Chill.

NOBODY IS
BETTER THAN ME!

NOBODY IS
WORSE.

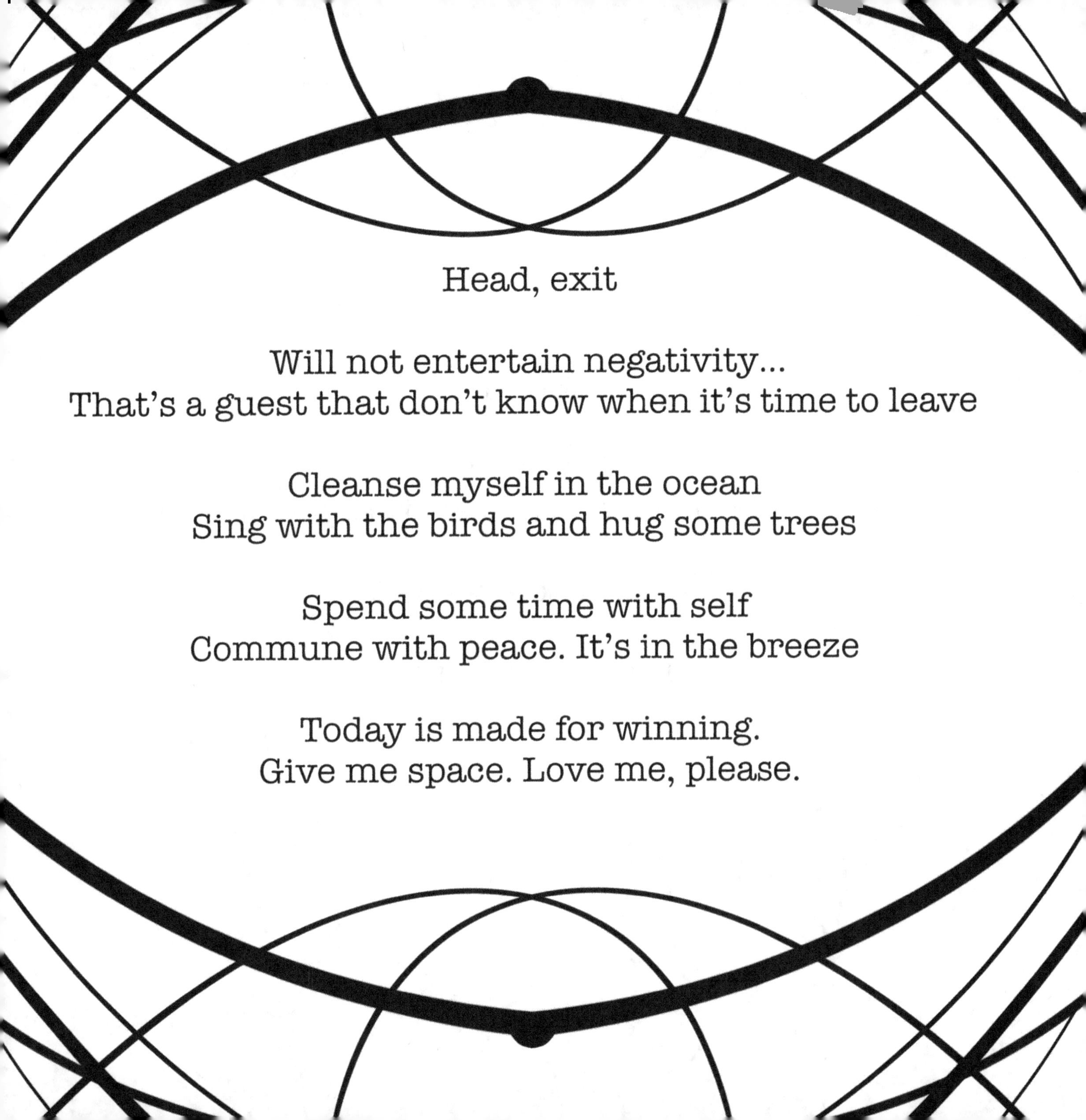
Head, exit

Will not entertain negativity...
That's a guest that don't know when it's time to leave

Cleanse myself in the ocean
Sing with the birds and hug some trees

Spend some time with self
Commune with peace. It's in the breeze

Today is made for winning.
Give me space. Love me, please.

Fresh

When I go
Please don't leave plastic flowers that never go away

I only came to visit

No one gets to stay

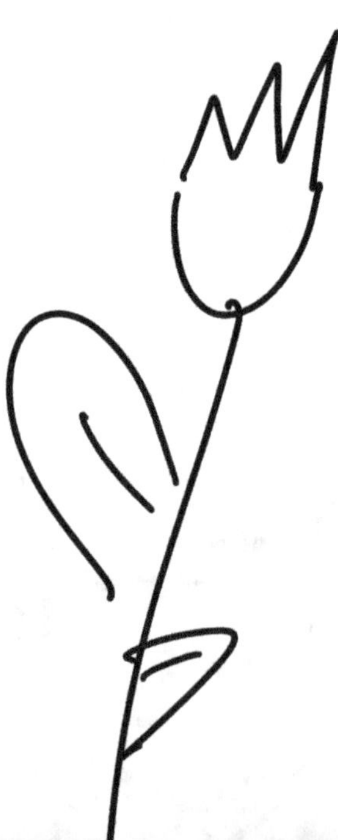

Down by the moon pond...
I dance free in the rain

Ancient waters electrify me
Complications turn to plains

Down by the moon pond...
Under an Aries sky...

I think about my father
I know the reason why

Down in the moon pond...
There was a blessing hidden
where I could not see

Long cycled precipitation
delivered
The message said to run away
and be free

Brick underpinning

Foundation I didn't realize existed

Foundation I didn't know I would need

Foundation that taught me to fight for it

Foundation taught me to succeed

Foundation that was brought into question

Foundation sound under a home with wheels?

Foundation closely analyzed

Foundation determined to be true & real.

CREATE

I am Augustus O. Brown Jr, a creative from Camden, SC.

Check out my other creations.

www.janiemaescosmicgarden.com